Is This "One of Those Days," Daddy?

Is This "One of Those Days," Daddy?

by Lynn Johnston

Andrews and McMeel, Inc.
A Universal Press Syndicate Company
Kansas City • New York

ISBN: 0-8362-1197-9
Library of Congress Catalog Card Number: 82-72417

First Printing, August 1982
Second Printing, September 1982
Third Printing, October 1982
Fourth Printing, December 1982
Fifth Printing, October 1983

One of the best parts of this job has been the many fine letters I've received from men and women who, but for the miles, could become cherished friends. My response to a fan letter two years ago has resulted in a sort of pen-pal bond between myself and a very talented, funny lady in Oakland, California, and as one busy mother to another (even busier mother) I imposed upon Alicia Anderson to write the foreword to this book.
—Lynn Johnston

A Word before the Best Part

A couple of years ago I wrote a fan letter. That was notable because I found the time. It's a matter of writing a line before changing the baby, after wiping the two-year-old's nose (without looking too closely), and between responses to my four-year-old's only known word: "Why?" My letter was to Lynn Johnston and I said something like, "You are drawing the story of my life!"

I wrote to her. "For Better or For Worse" was my answer to those people who think time hangs heavy on a mother's hands. She knows that the only thing that hangs heavy on a mother is a toddler. She understands the sensations a daddy feels when his joyful reception committee presents its peanut butter lips to be kissed. She knows that cat food is not fatal to small fry, that romantic evenings at home are a myth, and a mother's first gray hair is a war wound.

She understands parents. She also understands kids. She knows that a boy's idea of dressing up is a Hulk shirt and the jeans with one cuff out. She knows the heights of dignity a four-year-old can attain when reciting the alphabet. She knows what that expression of concentration on the baby's face *really* means.

One day, a childless friend, snugly stuffed into her designer jeans, dropped in on her way to somewhere else. This girl is pert (mothers are never pert) and said, pertly, "You never *do* anything!"

That's when I wrote the fan letter.

At my house, there are two goats and their six babies, eighteen chickens, three cats, two dogs, three kids under the age of five, and a man whose idea of a wild weekend is to scythe the backyard. At Lynn's house, there is one dog, two kids, and a dentist. No matter. "For Better or For Worse" is still the story of my life.

So go get a cup of coffee, sit down, and laugh. While the kids are taking their nap, of course.

—Alicia Anderson

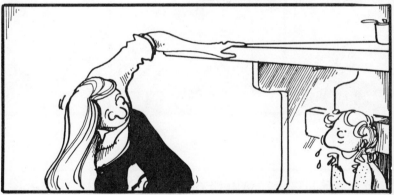

MY BROTHER'S COMING FOR CHRISTMAS, CONNIE!

YEAH, HE'S STILL WITH THE THEATRE, STILL PLAYING THE TRUMPET...

MARRIED? NO! — HE LEADS A CRAZY LIFE OF LATE NIGHTS, WOMEN, TRAVEL- -LING! — SOMEHOW HE STILL LIKES TO VISIT US WITH OUR KIDS, DOG AND MORTGAGE!

...I THINK IT CONVINCES HIM HE'S BEEN DOING THE RIGHT THING!

ELLY, I DON'T UNDERSTAND WHY I CAN'T LOSE WEIGHT!

FUN WITH WHEAT GERM

I BUY ALL NATURALLY GROWN ORGANIC PRODUCE... I DO MY OWN BAKING...

THE VICTORIOUS VITAMIN

HOW CAN ANYTHING SO HEALTHY BE SO FATTENING?

LOOK, ELLY... HOW ABOUT TRYING THIS NEWFANGLED DIET?

EAT THIN

WATERCRESS, CELERY, SPINACH, POACHED FISH, BOILED CHICKEN, PLAIN YOGOURT...

EAT THIN

IT SAYS THIS IS AN AWARD WINNING DIET. ...I WONDER WHY!

'CAUSE ANYONE WHO GOES THROUGH WITH IT DESERVES ONE.

OK, GROUP... IT'S DIET TIME!

STARTING TONIGHT WE COUNT OUR CALORIES ...AND YOU'LL ALL LEARN TO LIKE COTTAGE CHEESE!

BUT WE DON'T HAVE TO DIET— WE'RE FINE!

YEAH!

I KNOW... BUT I HATE TO SUFFER ALONE.

IF I HAVE TO EAT ANY MORE RABBIT FOOD... I'LL LEAVE HOME!

AND WHAT'S WITH THE DIET NOW?—WE'RE ONLY GOING TO GAIN IT ALL BACK OVER CHRIST-MAS!

BULGE

PASS THE LETTUCE

IS ANYBODY HOME?

UNCLE PHIL!

FAR OUT! WHO'S THE BIG DUDE?

WHICH SUITCASE HAS MY PRESENT IN —MMMFF?

OK... WE'LL JUST HELP YOU UNPACK!

22

SORRY I WAS SO LONG, EL — YOUR FRIEND ASKED ME IN!

LET'S SEE... WE DISCUSSED THE PRICE OF THEATRE TICKETS, THE FUTURE OF THE LARGE CAR AND THE JOYS OF WOK COOKING...

— SHE HAS FAIR LOOKS, GOOD LEGS, GOOD TEETH AND THE ONE THING WE HAVE IN COMMON IS AN ALLERGY TO DUST...

CUT IT OUT!

I KNOW YOU SET THIS UP, SIS... I'M JUST SAVING YOU HOURS OF BEATING 'ROUND THE BUSH!

Lynn

WHY ON EARTH WOULD YOU PLAY MATCHMAKER BETWEEN PHIL AND CONNIE?

THEY'RE A DISASTROUS COMBINATION! OIL AND WATER! TOTALLY WRONG FOR EACH OTHER!

I HOPE THEY KNOW THAT.

...THEY HAVE A DATE ON NEW YEAR'S EVE.

Lynn

5-4-3-2-1...

HAPPY NEW YEAR!

WELL, GIRL... LOOKS LIKE WE MADE IT THROUGH ANOTHER YEAR!

LET'S GO BACK TO BED, LIZ... THERE'S NOTHING SPECIAL ABOUT TONIGHT AFTER ALL.

Lynn

MY BROTHER IS SOMEWHERE WITH MY BEST FRIEND.... SO WHERE **ARE** THEY?

I BET HE'S SWEPT HER OFF HER FEET... I BET HE'S TAKING ADVANTAGE OF HER VULNERABILITY!

PACE PACE PACE

— HOW COULD HE DO THIS TO ME!!

SO WHERE THE HECK HAVE **YOU** BEEN?

I TOOK YOUR FRIEND CONNIE TO HER STAFF NEW YEARS' EVE PARTY.

— AND, SIS....

THAT'S ALL I'M GOING TO TELL YOU.

PAT PAT

Lynn

THE TROUBLE WITH CHRISTMAS HOLIDAYS IS THAT THEY'RE OVER TOO FAST!

YEAH.

SCHOOL ZONE

THE TROUBLE WITH CHRISTMAS HOLIDAYS IS THAT THEY LAST TOO LONG!

ACME SLIDE PROJECTOR

Lynn

25

I'VE GONE AND DONE IT NOW!

CONNIE THINKS MY BROTHER IS THE ANSWER TO HER DREAMS.

SHE REFUSES TO SEE HIM AS HE REALLY IS!

SOMETIMES THAT'S THE KEY TO A SUCCESSFUL RELATIONSHIP.

MOM? MOM? HEY...MOM?

MOM? MOM! **MOM!**

POKE POKE PAT

ROGET'S THESAURUS

MICHAEL, YOU ARE ASKING FOR A **SNACK!**

OH. I WAS HOPING FOR A HUG.

HOLY COW!—LOOK AT THE TEMPERATURE... AND IT'S SNOWING!

—STARK BARE BRANCHES AGAINST A CANVAS OF WHITE, GREY SKIES, ICY DRIFTS SCULPTURED BY THE WIND!

JOHN...WHY DON'T YOU SEE THE BEAUTY OF NATURE?

I'VE GOT TO GO OUT IN IT.

27

29

I HAVE A WEEK OFF —SO... I THOUGHT I'D GO TO MONTREAL!

JUST FOR A VISIT... A CHANGE... NO PARTICULAR REASON.

PHIL'S ADDRESS IS 271 RUE DES FÈVES.

THANKS, EL!

WOW! YOU GET TO STAY A WHOLE WEEK, LAWRENCE! YOU GET TO SLEEP IN MY ROOM AND EVERYTHING!

LAWRENCE IS STAYING— ISN'T THAT FANTASTIC, MOM?

...JUST WONDERFUL.

YOU BOYS STOP FOOLING AROUND AND GO TO SLEEP!

GIGGLE GIGGLE

OK—THAT'S IT! THIS IS YOUR LAST WARNING!

ONE MORE SOUND AND TWO PEOPLE WILL BE VERY SORRY!

SNICKER OOF! GIGGLE

US!

STAR WARS

I MEET HIM BY CHANCE AS I STROLL DOWN RUE DES FÈVES...

HE SMILES, WE TOUCH, THERE IN THE MIST I LOOK CHILDLIKE... INNOCENT.

I FEEL HELPLESS, WEAK, FEMININE... AND HE I... HONK!

SHADDUP YOU *!!6* MORON!

I MUST SAY YOU'VE BEEN AWFULLY GOOD TO CONNIE, EL...

YOU LISTEN TO HER, TAKE HER KID, LOOK AFTER HER HOUSE!

YOU'RE A VERY RELIABLE AND TRUE FRIEND!

YEAH.... I WISH I HAD A FRIEND LIKE ME!

MOM! - LIZZIE'S INTO EVERYTHING!

LAWRENCE AN' I CAN'T PLAY WITHOUT HER GETTING INTO OUR STUFF!

MICHAEL- YOU USUALLY PLAY SO WELL WITH YOUR LITTLE SISTER. SNIVEL

YEAH, BUT THAT'S WHEN I HAVEN'T GOT A CHOICE!

MY SON'S GOT A BROKEN LEG AND PHIL MAY BE LIVING WITH SOMEONE...

I SHOULD FORGET ABOUT PHIL, VISIT WITH FAMILY AND GO STRAIGHT HOME.

YES. THAT'S CERTAINLY GOOD ADVICE.

...I WONDER IF I'LL FOLLOW IT.

LOOK, EVERYONE AT SCHOOL SIGNED MY CAST!

AN' I DON'T HAFTA TAKE BATHS FOR A LONG TIME

I EVEN GET YOUR BED! THIS BROKEN LEG STUFF IS NEAT, MIKE!

TOO BAD IT DIDN'T HAPPEN TO SOMEBODY ELSE.

I'M NOT GOING TO LET FATE SPOIL THINGS. IF MY COUSIN CAN'T SEE PHIL PERFORM TONIGHT... I'LL GO ALONE.

HE WON'T EVEN KNOW I'M THERE. I'LL BE A SECRET, INVISIBLE ADMIRER.

NO, HEH... I'M ALONE. I'M A FRIEND OF SOMEONE IN THE BAND.

IN THAT CASE, WE HAVE ONE SEAT LEFT - RIGHT IN FRONT.

ELLY, YOU'VE BEEN JUST GREAT TO US! THANKYOU, THANKYOU!

THANKS FOR TAKING CARE OF LAWRENCE!

I REALLY CAN'T THANK YOU ENOUGH.

BOY. ...I'D SAY SHE THANKED YOU ENOUGH!

I MUST MAKE A MENTAL NOTE TO PAY THIS BILL...

AND I'VE MADE MENTAL NOTES TO CALL THE DRUG STORE AND DROP OFF THE CLOTHES LAWRENCE LEFT.

MOM?—HOWCOME DADDY'S ALWAYS MAKING MENTAL NOTES?

IT'S THE ONLY WAY HE CAN READ HIS OWN WRITING!

THEY LET ME BE LAWRENCE'S "SPECIAL FRIEND" AT SCHOOL.

I GET TO HELP HIM WITH HIS BOOKS AN' COAT AN' STUFF.

MOM, HOWCOME IT HAD TO BE LAWRENCE THAT BROKE HIS LEG?

I THOUGHT THOSE THINGS ALWAYS HAPPENED TO PEOPLE YOU DON'T KNOW!

SIT, FARLEY
SIT, FARLEY
SIT, FARLEY
SIT!

SIT
SIT
SIT
SI —

YARF!

SO, I HEAR THAT LAWRENCE GOT THE CAST OFF HIS LEG TODAY!

YEAH. WE WANTED HIM TO BRING IT IN FOR SHOW AN' TELL.

HE SAYS HIS LEG FEELS FUNNY, BUT HE CAN WALK FINE...

HE JUST WON'T BE ABLE TO KICK ANYONE FOR AWHILE.

MICHAEL — I ASKED YOU TO PICK UP THESE TOYS AGES AGO!

ARE YOU TWO FIGHTING AGAIN?

LOOK, HONEY... WE CAN ENROLL THE DOG IN AN OBEDIENCE TRAINING CLASS!

GREAT... I WONDER IF THEY ACCEPT CHILDREN.

40

FARLEY'S GOING TO SCHOOL! FARLEY'S SUCH A BIG, BIG BOY!

HE'S GOING TO BE DADDY'S GOOOD PUPPY! HE'S GOING TO DO EVERYTHING DADDY SAYS!

WOULDN'T IT BE JUST AS REASSURING IF HE CALLED ME BY MY FIRST NAME?

NOW, YOUR FIRST TOOL IN OBEDIENCE TRAINING IS PRAISE!

PRAISE IS OF UTMOST IMPORTANCE. I CANNOT STRESS THIS ENOUGH!

WELL, HOW DO YOU THINK WE DID?

YOU WERE WONDERFUL, HONEY, JUST WONDERFUL!

NOW, MIKE—YOU'RE THE BOSS. YOU LET FARLEY KNOW HIS LIMITS, SEE?

JUST SAY HEEL AS YOU PULL UP SMARTLY ON THE LEASH, AND YOUR DOG WILL AUTO-MATICALLY—

HEEL!!

42

I SAID "MY MONEY," DIDN'T I. ....I SAID THE WRONG THING.

I SHOULD HAVE SAID "OUR MONEY." I SHOULD HAVE ASKED YOU IF I COULD BUY THE STEREO ....SHOULDN'T I ...

GROWL

IT'S GOOD TO KNOW WE CAN STILL COMMUNICATE.

Lynn

I DON'T BELIEVE IT! I GO WITHOUT A $20⁰⁰ CAN OPENER TO SAVE A FEW DOLLARS ....

AND WHO GOES OUT AND SPENDS A **FORTUNE** ON SOMETHING WE DON'T NEED?

WHAT'S THE POINT IN TRYING TO BE FRUGAL? WHY BUDGET —WHY?

WHO WAS IT WHO SAID "TO BE BORN IS TO SUFFER"?

Lynn

YOU'RE RIGHT—IT'S AN EXPENSIVE STEREO.

BUT IT'S GREAT QUALITY.—THE BEST!

AND IF I DIDN'T GO FOR THE BEST, I WOULDN'T HAVE MARRIED YOU!

IT WON'T WORK, PATTERSON !!

Lynn

I DON'T UNDERSTAND IT, ANNE. HOW CAN HE RATIONALIZE THAT MUCH MONEY ON A TOY FOR HIMSELF?

YOU'RE NOT SO BAD OFF- DIDN'T HE GET YOU A TRASH COMPACTOR FOR CHRISTMAS?

TRASH COMPACTOR! WHY WOULD I WANT A TRASH COMPACTOR?

— I MARRIED A MAN WITH SIZE 12 FEET!

"OUR MONEY" REALLY IS HIS MONEY. I DON'T EARN A CENT.

I KNOW THAT'S THE WRONG ATTITUDE. THERE MUST BE AN OBVIOUS WAY TO PROVE MY MONETARY WORTH.

THAT WAS A BURP. GREAT SUPPER, ELLY!

FINE. THAT'S $15.95, WITH TAX AND 30¢ FOR THE COFFEE.

SO NOW I'VE TOLD YOU THE WHOLE STORY. ELLY'S STILL MAD AT ME. I JUST WISH I KNEW HOW TO HANDLE IT!

I HINK OOH HOOD HAKE ACK UH HEREO. — AT OOD HIX HINGS UF!

THAT'S EASY FOR YOU TO SAY!

A DISHWASHER?- JOHN... I DON'T BELIEVE IT!!

YOU'RE JUSTIFYING BUYING THAT EXPENSIVE STEREO BY GETTING ME A DISHWASHER!!

YOU WANT ME TO TAKE IT BACK?

NO.

I GUESS EVERYONE HAS HER PRICE...

IT'S COLD AN' IT'S RAINING AN' I'VE GOT NOTHING TO DO!

WELL, MIKE, YOU COULD TIDY YOUR ROOM, BRUSH THE DOG, STRAIGHTEN THE BOOTS...

AW, MOM - I DON'T WANNA DO DUMB CHORES AROUND THE HOUSE! - I WANNA DO SOMETHING THAT'S FUN!

... I KNOW THE FEELING.

LOOK, ANNE... I'M TEMPTED TO BUY SOME OF THIS "LOOK YOUNGER" FORMULA.

I'M NOT! - I'VE GOT THE BEST LOOK-YOUNGER FORMULA IN THE WORLD!

LEAVE THE KIDS WITH GRANDMA!

DR. N. PLETT
PHYSICIAN & SURGEON

SNIVEL

WE'LL SEE ELIZABETH NOW, MRS. PATTERSON.

YAH!

HER GLANDS ARE UP, SHE'S GOT SOME TONSILLITIS AND A TOUCH OF OTITIS MEDIA-

I THINK.

THE REASON LIZZIE GETS SICK, ELLY, IS BECAUSE YOU DON'T GIVE HER THE RIGHT FOODS.

CHRISTOPHER DOESN'T EAT ANYTHING UNLESS I KNOW EXACTLY WHERE IT'S FROM, WHAT'S IN IT AND...

HEALTH BUDS

HEY,-MOM!-CHRIS AN' LIZZIE ARE IN THE GARDEN EATIN' DIRT!

BUT, ANNE... IT'S ORGANIC!

HELP YOURSELF, EL... I'VE GOT EVERY BOOK ON CHILD-RAISING THERE IS!

THANKS, ANNE... BUT I'VE ALWAYS PICKED UP ADVICE FROM MY MOM!

YOUR MOTHER! - I'D NEVER ASK MY MOM ANYTHING ABOUT CHILD RAISING.

- SHE DID IT ALL WRONG.

I'M SURPRISED YOU'RE SO OLD-FASHIONED, ELLY!

HAVEN'T YOU TRIED T.A. OR PARENT EFFECTIVENESS TRAINING?

WATCH: - CHRISTOPHER, MOMMY GETS ANGRY WHEN MILK IS SPILLED ON THE FLOOR, ... MOMMY..

'DUMP! -

HOLY COW, ELLY, THERE'S A COUPLE OF WOMEN WRESTLERS ON T.V.!

NOW WHAT DO YOU SUPPOSE WOULD MAKE A COUPLE OF WOMEN WANT TO FIGHT LIKE THAT?!

ONE PROBABLY TOLD THE OTHER SHE DIDN'T KNOW HOW TO RAISE HER KIDS.

UROOM... UROOOMMMM!

TRUCK. CAR. CAR. CAR.

RRUMMF.. SLAM!

THERE. THAT'S OUR CAR.

CLICK..STEP STEP..STEP...

CREEK...

YOU DIDN'T REALLY APPRECIATE ME GOING OUT ON THE TOWN LAST NIGHT, DID YOU?

-BUT IT'S PERFECTLY ALL RIGHT FOR YOU TO GO OUT 'TILL ALL HOURS WITH "THE BOYS"!

THAT'S DIFFERENT.

WHEN I'M OUT....I KNOW WHERE YOU ARE!

JOHN, WHY DON'T YOU THROW OUT THOSE AWFUL CHECKED PANTS?

THEY'RE COMFORTABLE.

BESIDES...IT'S ME WHO'S WALKING AROUND IN THEM, NOT YOU!

- BUT I'M THE ONE WHO GETS BLAMED.

WHO IN THE WORLD WROTE UP THIS CLAIM FORM?

... LOOKS LIKE YOUR WRITING.

ARE YOU KIDDING? -THIS DECREPIT SCRAWL IS ABSOLUTELY <u>PRIMITIVE</u>! MY WRITING IS <u>NOT</u> PRIMITIVE!

-IT'S JUST ILLEGIBLE.

THUMP! CRASH! BANG! BANG THUMP! BUMP

CUT IT OUT!!!

SO MUCH FOR THE PITTER PATTER OF LITTLE FEET.

DESPITE YOUR COMPLAINTS, I THINK WOMEN AT HOME ARE LUCKY.

WHAT? CHASING KIDS, COOKING, CLEANING, SHOPPING...

I REALLY DON'T SEE WHAT THERE IS TO ENVY ABOUT OUR LOT!

YOU HAVE THE TIME TO MAKE FRIENDS.

IT'S TRUE! WHEN DO I HAVE TIME FOR FRIENDSHIPS?

I SEE PEOPLE ALL DAY — BUT I NEVER HAVE TIME TO REALLY TALK TO THEM.

SOMETIMES I THINK I'M ACTUALLY LONELY.

HERE, DADDY.

THERE WAS ONCE A TIME WHEN I HAD A "BEST FRIEND." DON'T YOU REMEMBER HAVING A BEST FRIEND, ELLY?

UH HUH. — IN FACT I STILL HAVE A BEST FRIEND.

YOU.

AH HAH! FLOWERS FOR THE WEE WIFEY!

HI, TED.

SO, WHAT DID YOU DO, TIE ONE ON? COME IN LATE?

NO... I JUST THOUGHT I'D DO SOMETHING NICE.

CLINIC ENTRANCE

YOU HAPPILY MARRIED TYPES ARE NO FUN!

SURE..ER...FINE — YOU CAN BRING TED HOME FOR SUPPER, JOHN.

POT LUCK? YEAH. I GUESS YOU COULD TELL HIM IT'S POT LUCK.

— ACTUALLY IT'S MORE LIKE "EAT AT YOUR OWN RISK."

YESSIR...YOU'VE GOT YOURSELF A FINE LITTLE COOK THERE, JOHN!

— A MAN NEEDS PAMPERING ONCE IN A WHILE...

AND THERE'S NOTHING LIKE A WOMAN TO GIVE IT TO HIM.

I THINK I'M ABOUT TO GIVE IT TO HIM.

TED, DO YOU REALLY THINK WOMEN WERE PUT ON THIS EARTH TO SERVE MEN?

WE ARE EQUALS!

IF I COOK AND CLEAN IT'S BECAUSE I CHOOSE TO DO SO — NOT BECAUSE I AM SUBSERVIENT!

YOU DIDN'T TELL ME SHE WAS "ONE OF THOSE."

66

LIZZIE. AS OF TODAY... YOU ARE OFFICIALLY TOO BIG FOR THE BACK-PACK.

Jynn

NO. YOU'RE A BIG GIRL, ELIZABETH. YOU CAN WALK.

BYE BYE, THEN. MOMMY'S GOING.

Jynn

I DON'T CARE ABOUT MY HEART CONDITION, NEIL... I WANT THIS BABY!

BUT I CAN'T MARRY YOU, BARBARA.. MY WIFE IS IN A COMA THIS WEEK AND CAN'T SIGN THE DIVORCE PAPERS!

WHAT DRIVEL. WHAT COMPLETE AND UTTER TRASH!

OH... SOB SNIVEL

YEAH. WHO'D EVER BOTHER WATCHING IT.

Jynn

IT'S SUCH A LOVELY DAY, I COULD SIT HERE FOREVER!

TOO BAD OUR HUSBANDS ARE STUCK IN THEIR OFFICES!

WELL—BETTER GO GET DINNER ON. YEAH. SEE YOU, ANNE.

GUILT IS A GREAT MOTIVATOR, ELIZABETH.

CONNIE—IF YOUR SITTER IS SICK I'D BE GLAD TO HAVE LAWRENCE COME HERE!

SURE HE CAN PLAY WITH MICHAEL 'TILL YOU GET HOME!

DON'T BE SILLY—I EXPECT YOU TO ASK ME FOR FAVORS LIKE THIS.

IT'S ONE OF THE HAZARDS OF NOT WORKING.

MOM, HOWCOME LAWRENCE HAS TO GO TO A SITTER EVERY DAY?

— BECAUSE HIS MOM HAS TO WORK, MICHAEL.

SHE WORKS SO THAT SHE CAN PAY FOR THEIR HOUSE, FOOD, CLOTHES—EVERYTHING!

BUT WHY DOESN'T SHE JUST GET MONEY FROM THE BANK LIKE EVERYONE ELSE?

COME ON, MIKE, WHO'S GONNA KNOW?

I'LL SHOW YOU MINE IF YOU SHOW ME YOURS....

REPORT CARDS.

Michael's academic work is normal. He would excel if he settled down.

Social skills are coming slowly. He is learning to control his active nature.

He has shown an aptitude for athletics, group leadership and public speaking.

It is with great ~~belief~~ pleasure that I promote Michael to grade two.

GOODBYE, MISS CAMPBELL. I'M SORRY I WAS THE BADDEST KID IN CLASS.

WHY, MICHAEL!

YOU WEREN'T BAD! WITHOUT YOU, IT WOULD HAVE BEEN A PRETTY DULL YEAR... AND I'M REALLY GOING TO MISS YOU!

THAT'S GOTTA BE THE BEST SORRY I EVER SAID.

LOOK, MA! MRS. BAIRD JUST GAVE US AN ICE CREAM BAR!

GREAT.

WHAT'S WRONG, MOM?...

MRS. BAIRD ALWAYS GIVES US THIS KINDA STUFF!

...AND ALWAYS EXACTLY 10 MINUTES BEFORE SUPPER.

ANNE, I'VE ASKED MRS. BAIRD SEVERAL TIMES NOT TO FEED MY KIDS BEFORE DINNER!

I KNOW SHE MEANS WELL—BUT SHE KEEPS DOING IT ...AND IT'S DRIVING ME CRAZY!

YOU'RE NOT COMMUNICATING. CAN'T YOU BE A LITTLE MORE EXPLICIT ABOUT YOUR FEELINGS?

I COULD BLOW UP HER FRIDGE.

WHAT ARE YOU STARING AT?

I'D FORGOTTEN YOU HAD LEGS.

71

DO YOU EVER HEAR FROM YOUR BROTHER, ELLY?

OH, SURE - HE'S BUSY TEACHING NOW. HE HAS 6 TRUMPET STUDENTS.

I WISH HE COULD TEACH ME A FEW THINGS...

I CAN'T PLAY A NOTE... BUT I CAN PUCKER.

YOU STILL THINK ABOUT PHIL A LOT DON'T YOU, CONNIE.

OF COURSE. WHEN THERE'S NOTHING NEW ON THE HORIZON - YOU HANG ONTO WHATEVER YOU HAD - EVEN IF YOU NEVER HAD IT.

YOU'RE NUT'S!

YOU HAVEN'T BEEN SINGLE FOR AWHILE HAVE YOU, ELLY?

WHERE YOU GOING FOR YOUR HOLIDAYS, MICHAEL?

THIS FRIEND OF MY DAD'S IS LENDIN' US HIS CABIN! THERE'S A LAKE, AN' BOATS AN' FISH AN' EVERYTHING!

WHAT'RE YOU GONNA DO?

I THINK MY MOM'S GONNA LET ME MAKE A TENT IN THE BACK YARD!

HERE'S THE MAP TED DREW UP, AND THE KEYS TO HIS CABIN.

GREAT. THEN EVERYTHING'S READY BUT THE SURVIVAL KIT.

SURVIVAL KIT? THE PLACE IS FULLY EQUIPPED! WHAT IS THERE TO SURVIVE?

THE TWO-DAY DRIVE IT TAKES TO GET THERE.

WE DON'T SEE EACH OTHER EVERY DAY, ELLY, BUT I'M GOING TO MISS YOU!

WE'RE ONLY GOING AWAY FOR TWO WEEKS.

I KNOW. STILL... THE NEIGHBORHOOD CHANGES SOMEHOW.

ARE YOU TALKING ABOUT THE NOISE LEVEL OR THE PROPERTY VALUES?

INSTEAD OF LEAVING YOUR PLACE EMPTY, JOHN — WHY DON'T I LOOK AFTER IT?

BUT YOU LIVE WITH YOUR MOTHER — WOULDN'T SHE MIND?

MIND! — SHE **WANTS** ME TO MOVE OUT!

SHE SAYS I'M CRAMPING HER STYLE.

DON'T WORRY ABOUT MY PLANTS, ANNIE... TED'S GOING TO HOUSESIT WHILE WE'RE AWAY!

YES, THE ONE WITH THE CABIN. YES, HE STILL LIVES WITH HIS MOTHER....

—WELL, BECAUSE HE HASN'T FOUND THE RIGHT GIRL YET.

TO BEGIN WITH— HE'S BEEN LOOKING IN THE WRONG CENTURY.

I'M LOOKING FORWARD TO THIS VACATION AND HAVING TIME TOGETHER, ELLY.

AS WELL AS BEING PARENTS, I WANT THE KIDS TO SEE US AS REAL, BASIC HUMAN BEINGS!

HONEY, IF 2 WEEKS IN THE BUSH WITH A WOOD STOVE AND AN OUTHOUSE WON'T DO IT...

NOTHING WILL.

—HERE IT IS... MY TRUSTY OLD BIKINI.

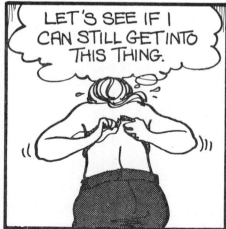

LET'S SEE IF I CAN STILL GET INTO THIS THING.

...AMAZING WHAT ONE CAN DO WITH STRETCH FABRIC.

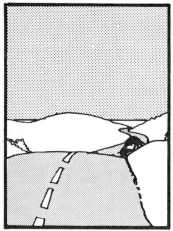

WELL, THIS IS OUR LAST NIGHT HERE... AND YOU'VE GOT TO ADMIT— WE'VE BEEN A REAL FAMILY.

IT TAKES AN ADVENTURE LIKE THIS TO BRING US ALL CLOSER TOGETHER!

YEAH. IT'S BEEN THE ONLY WAY TO KEEP FROM FREEZING TO DEATH.

LYNN

OK, THE CAR'S PACKED, EVERYBODY— LET'S GO!

HERE, FARLEY, COME ON, BOY!

WOOF!

LYNN

COULDN'T YOU JUST WASH THE SKUNK OFF FARLEY, MA? DID YOU HAFTA SHAVE HIM TOO?

I DON'T KNOW IF I CAN LIVE WITH A BALD DOG!

MICHAEL... IF YOU WANT TO LIVE TO SEE ANOTHER BIRTHDAY...

YOU'LL KEEP QUIET.

LYNN

80

COME ON, ELLY... IN SPITE OF THE LOUSY CABIN, THE SKUNK AND THE FLIES... SURELY YOU CAN SAY SOMETHING GOOD ABOUT OUR TRIP!

WOOF

YEAH. - NEXT YEAR *I* DECIDE WHERE WE GO FOR A HOLIDAY!

OK, WE'RE HOME - AND TED'S CAR IS IN THE DRIVEWAY.

WE'RE GOING TO TELL HIM THANKS FOR THE USE OF THE CABIN...

WE'RE GOING TO SAY WHAT A GREAT TIME WE HAD...

IN OTHER WORDS... WE'RE GONNA LIE THROUGH OUR TEETH.

SO YOU FOLKS LIKED MY LITTLE WILDERNESS HIDEAWAY!

DID YOU USE THE FIREPLACE? THE SUN-PORCH? THE SAUNA?

YOU IDIOT!! - WE WERE AT THE *WRONG* CABIN!

AT LEAST TED KEPT THE HOUSE IN GOOD SHAPE, ELLY!

...YOU'RE NOT SPEAKING TO ME— RIGHT?

WELL...MAYBE I'D BETTER ENJOY THE SILENCE— WHILE IT LASTS.

WHAP!

HEY, MICHAEL!—YOU'RE BACK!— DIDJA HAVE A GOOD TIME?

WHAT'S THE MATTER? I DUNNO

MY MOM'S MAD AT MY DAD AND THEY'RE NOT SPEAKING TO EACH OTHER.

—BUT THEY'RE BOTH YELLING AT ME!

ELLY— I DON'T CARE HOW ANGRY YOU ARE ... I LOVE YOU.

I DON'T CARE WHAT YOU'RE ANGRY ABOUT — I LOVE YOU!

I DON'T CARE IF YOU WON'T TALK... I STILL LOVE YOU.

THIS IS THE ONLY WAY TO FIGHT.

IT WAS **YOU** WHO TOOK CARE OF OUR HOUSE WHILE WE WERE AWAY!

—I NOTICED TEDDY WAS HAVING TROUBLE DOING DISHES AND THINGS SO...

CONNIE! AFTER ALL YOUR LECTURES ABOUT MEN BEING ABLE TO LOOK AFTER THEMSELVES!

BUT ELLY... SOME OF THEM ARE SO HELPLESS!

WELL··IT SEEMS SHE CAME OVER TO BORROW THE LAWN-MOWER, AND IT WAS LOVE AT FIRST **BURP**.

JUST A MINUTE, ANNIE.... **BURP** GIGGLE **BRAACK BELCH·· BURRP**

MICHAEL—HANG UP THE EXTENSION PHONE **OR ELSE!**

NEVER HAVE KIDS.

ELLY, CONNIE AND TED'S SUDDEN RELATIONSHIP IS THEIR BUSINESS.

WHATEVER GOES ON BETWEEN THEM IS NO CONCERN OF OURS.

THEY ARE OUR FRIENDS—AND WE HAVE NO RIGHT TO PRY.

....BUT IF YOU FIND OUT ANYTHING — LET ME KNOW.

SPRING! BOUNCE!

MICHAEL! — DO **NOT** TREAT MY FURNITURE LIKE THAT!!

A COUCH IS TO SIT ON! IT IS NOT A TRAMPOLINE! FURNITURE COSTS MONEY!

SIGH .. ANOTHER DAY .... ANOTHER LECTURE.

THERE'S NOTHIN' TO DO, THERE'S NOTHIN' ON T.V., THERE'S NOTHIN' TO PLAY WITH, THERE'S NOBODY AROUND.

MICHAEL — THERE'S <u>ALWAYS</u> SOMETHING TO DO. LIFE'S TOO SHORT TO WASTE A SECOND OF IT!

YOU SHOULD READ A STORY — OR MAKE SOMETHING. — I THINK TIME IS PRECIOUS!

THAT'S 'CAUSE YOU DON'T HAVE AS MUCH LEFT AS I DO.

BACK TO SCHOOL SPECIAL

WHAT'S SO SPECIAL ABOUT BACK TO SCHOOL, MOM?

MOM?

I DON'T WANT YOU USING THOSE SUPPLIES, MICHAEL— THEY'RE FOR SCHOOL

NO, YOU CAN'T WEAR THOSE CLOTHES. —THEY'RE FOR SCHOOL!

HOWCOME I CAN'T USE MY SCHOOL STUFF **NOW**??

IT'S ONLY GOING TO LOOK NICE FOR ONE DAY ANYHOW.

MICHAEL! WHAT HAVE YOU PEOPLE DONE TO YOUR PUPPY?

OH, MY POOR WITTLE DOGGUMS! WHAT HAS MOMMY DONE? SHE'S CUT OFF ALL HIS HAIR, POOR BABY!

MRS BAIRD'S A LITTLE WEIRD. INSTEAD OF HAVIN' KIDS, SHE HAD PUPPIES.

BOY, AM I EXHAUSTED. —MRS BAIRD CAME OVER TODAY AND NEVER STOPPED TALKING!

SHE GOES ON AND ON NONSTOP, JOHN— IT REALLY WEARS ME OUT!

AND WHAT BUGS ME IS THAT SHE TALKS ABOUT NOTHING!

YOU SHOULD BE ABLE TO HANDLE THAT!

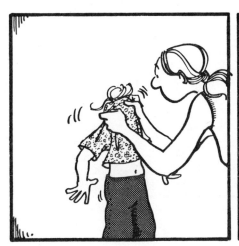

MICHAEL, TED AND CONNIE ARE COMING FOR SUPPER, AND I WANT YOU TO WASH YOUR HANDS.

THEN I WANT YOU TO GO AND PUT ON A CLEAN SHIRT.

DO I WASH FOR SHORT SLEEVES OR LONG ?!

THAT WAS A GREAT SUPPER, ELLY! — LET ME HELP YOU CLEAN UP.

TIMES HAVEN'T CHANGED, TED...

THE MEN RETIRE TO THE LIVINGROOM TO TALK ABOUT WORK....

AND THE WOMEN GO INTO THE KITCHEN — —AND TALK ABOUT US.

YOU HAD SUCH A LONG LIST OF THINGS YOU WANTED IN A MAN, CONNIE....

IT'S AMAZING YOU TWO HIT IT OFF SO WELL!

DOES TED REALLY MATCH UP TO ALL THOSE REQUIREMENTS?

I CHANGED THE LIST.

I'M TELLING YOU, JOHN— LIFE IS GREAT!

— HOME COOKING, FUN WITH THE KID, A LOVING LADY....

CONNIE'S A VERY SPECIAL FRIEND, TED.

WHAT'S THIS? ARE YOU ASKING IF MY INTENTIONS ARE HONORABLE?

lynn

WELL, I'D SAY IT'S BEEN A GREAT EVENING!

TAKE CARE, YOU TWO—

KEEP IN TOUCH.

IF YOU EVER NEED ANYTHING, WE'RE HERE.

THANKS, MOM.

lynn

I THINK THAT TED GENUINELY CARES FOR CONNIE— BUT SHE'S IN TOO MUCH OF A FOG TO SEE ANYTHING!

YEAH. I PREDICT THEY'LL HAVE SOME ROUGH TIMES AFTER THE INFATUATION WEARS OFF!

... ISN'T IT AMAZING HOW WE CAN BE SO OBJECTIVE ABOUT OTHER PEOPLE'S RELATIONSHIPS....

— AND SO NAIVE ABOUT OUR OWN!

lynn

ALL RIGHT— AS NEAR AS I CAN FIGURE IT, YOU HAVE A TOTAL OF $129⁰⁰....

AND NO CENTS.

JUST LET MOMMY FINISH THIS PAGE, SWEETHEART.

JUST THIS ONE PAGE AND THEN WE'LL GO OUT.

ALL I HAVE TO DO IS ONE PAGE, ELIZABETH!

AND THEY WONDER WHY WE NEVER GET ANYTHING DONE!

HEY, MA....LIZZIE'S LOST HER GUM AGAIN!

WELL, HERE IT IS. — THE SEASON THAT I HATE.

COME ON, ANNE! THE KIDS ARE IN SCHOOL, THE AIR'S COOL, THE LEAVES ARE TURNING...

I'M NOT TALKING ABOUT AUTUMN, DUMMY!

I'M TALKING ABOUT FOOTBALL.

WHY DO PEOPLE WATCH FOOTBALL ANYWAYS?

ALL IT IS—IS A BUNCH OF PADDED UP MEN BENDING OVER!

THEY RUN AROUND, THEY FALL DOWN, AND THEN IT'S ANOTHER VIEW OF REAR ENDS!

...SO...YOU AND STEVE SEE THE SITUATION FROM DIFFERENT ANGLES!

IF STEVE LIKES FOOTBALL THAT MUCH, ANNE, MAYBE YOU COULD GET INTERESTED IN IT TOO!

YEAH, I SUPPOSE SO.

EXCEPT I'M ALWAYS SO BUSY SERVING THE GUYS HE INVITES OVER...

I NEVER SIT DOWN LONG ENOUGH TO LEARN ANYTHING

MICHAEL, YOU'RE NOT TOO YOUNG TO DO SOME WORK AROUND HERE!

IN FACT — YOU OWE IT TO US!

WE PAY FOR YOUR CLOTHES, YOUR FOOD, YOUR EDUCATION...

DID I ASK TO GET BORN?

JOHN — DID YOU HAVE TO SPANK MICHAEL?

GRUMBLE SNARL...

SURELY THERE'S SOME OTHER WAY TO HANDLE HIM!

YOU'VE GOT A DEGREE IN PSYCHOLOGY — WHAT DID YOU STUDY ALL THOSE YEARS?

RATS, MOSTLY.

WOW, MIKE — YOU'RE RAKIN' LEAVES!

YOU DOIN' IT BECAUSE YOU HAVE TO?

NOPE — I'M DOIN' IT 'CAUSE I WANT TO!

I'LL COME BACK WHEN YOU'RE FEELIN' BETTER.

THIS PAYMENT IS PAST DUE. REMIT AMOUNT SHOWN IMMEDIATELY OR SERVICE WILL BE DISCONTINUED.

LOOK AT THIS AWFUL NOTICE. I DON'T DESERVE THIS! —I'VE BEEN AN EXCELLENT CUSTOMER!

THEY NEVER COMMEND YOU FOR PAYING ON TIME — BUT SLIP UP ONCE AND YOU GET INSULTED!

JUST SEE IF I USE THE TELEPHONE AGAIN !!!

HELLO— I'M CALLING ABOUT A VERY RUDE "PAYMENT OVERDUE" NOTICE.

WITH THIS ONE EXCEPTION, I'VE ALWAYS PAID ON TIME —BUT YOUR REMINDER TREATS ME LIKE A CREDIT RISK! A THIEF!

IS THAT ANY WAY TO TREAT A GOOD CUSTOMER ?... HUH ? ER,...OK. THANKS.

SHE SAID SHE'D HAVE A HARSH WORD WITH THEIR COMPUTER.

MICHAEL, THIS IS A LIVINGROOM !!!

I KNOW ...WE'RE LIVIN' IN IT.

JUST 'CAUSE GORDON'S IN GRADE 3, JUST 'CAUSE HE'S A NEW KID, JUST 'CAUSE HE'S GOT GUM... MICHAEL LIKES HIM BETTER.

MICHAEL IS A RAT FINK. MICHAEL IS A NERD FACE. IF I EVER SEE MICHAEL AGAIN....

WHATEVER IT IS THAT'S UPSETTING YOU, HONEY-COULDN'T BE THAT BAD.

WHAT DO YOU KNOW. YOU HAVEN'T BEEN A KID FOR YEARS!

THE WAY I SEE IT.... MICHAEL HAS A NEW FRIEND, AND LAWRENCE FEELS LOST AND LEFT OUT.

EVEN TED-WHO'S A DOCTOR-CAN'T FIGURE OUT WHY HE'S TAKING IT SO HARD!

YOU'VE BEEN SEEING TED EVERY DAY FOR WEEKS... HAVEN'T YOU, CONNIE.

MAYBE IT'S NOT A BEST FRIEND HE FEELS HE'S LOST... MAYBE IT'S YOU!

LAWRENCE...I WANT YOU TO KNOW THAT YOU ARE THE MOST PRECIOUS THING IN MY LIFE.

...I MIGHT FALL IN LOVE WITH SOMEONE GROWN UP BECAUSE I'M LONELY AND I NEED A PARTNER.

BUT, NOBODY-NOBODY COULD TAKE YOUR PLACE. NOT EVER. YOU'RE PART OF ME. YOU'RE EXTRA SPECIAL.

AND SO ARE MOMENTS LIKE THESE!

I CAN'T DO THIS, I WON'T DO IT! I **HATE** THIS! - IT'S NOT FAIR!!

WHAT'S WITH HIM?

THE USUAL....

FOR EVERY 10 MINUTES OF HOMEWORK, THERE'S A HALF HOUR OF COMPLAINTS.

WE'RE SURE LUCKY, JOHN. HERE WE ARE AFTER 9 YEARS OF MARRIAGE...

AND WE'RE STILL HAPPY! - STILL TOGETHER.

I ATTRIBUTE IT TO REAL COMPATIBILITY.

AND THE FACT THAT I CAN'T SEE A THING WITHOUT MY GLASSES.

GOOD GRIEF! - IT'S MIDNIGHT!

BUT... WE WERE JUST BEGINNING TO UNDERSTAND OUR RELATIONSHIP!

WHY DO WE ALWAYS GET INTO LONG DISCUSSIONS AFTER WE'RE IN BED?!

IT'S THE ONLY TIME WE SEE EACH OTHER.

YOU GOING BACK TO THAT NIGHT SCHOOL, MOM?

UH HUH

HOW COME?

I WANT TO IMPROVE MY MIND!

NIGHTSCHOOL IS A MEANS OF EXPANSION, A MEANS OF REAWAKENING ONE'S TALENTS:

— A MEANS OF ESCAPE....

I'M LATE! NOW WHERE THE HECK IS THAT DUMB, STUPID RM. 416?

32F

HEH HEH - OOPS, EXCUSE ME - PARDON ME...

OW! —DUMB NYLONS! — I'VE RIPPED MY LOUSY STUPID CRUMMY CHEAP **NYLONS!**

GOOD EVENING, CLASS — WELCOME TO 'ENGLISH, OUR CREATIVE LANGUAGE.'

WHO, ME? — ER — I FEEL THAT A WRITER MUST ALSO BE AN ENTERTAINER.

HUH? YES, THIS ESPECIALLY APPLIES TO NEWSPAPER REPORTING.

HOW LONG HAVE I BEEN AN AVID SUBSCRIBER TO A DAILY NEWSPAPER?

LET'S SEE... HOW OLD IS THE DOG....

MOM, MY PHYS ED. TEACHER COACHES HOCKEY!—CAN I PLAY? NO.

BUT LAWRENCE IS JOINING AN' GORDON AN' EVERYONE! NO.

HE SAYS WE'LL LEARN SPORTSMANSHIP AN' TEAM SPIRIT, AN' DISCIPLINE! WELL...

GREAT. I ALREADY ORDERED MY UNIFORM!

HOLY COW! IT'S GOING TO COST US A FORTUNE TO OUTFIT YOU FOR HOCKEY!

AND LOOK AT YOUR SCHEDULE! JOHN—LOOK AT THE COST AND THE SCHEDULE!

SIGH.. I PLAYED HOCKEY WHEN I WAS A KID...

CASE CLOSED.

TED WANTS LAWRENCE TO PLAY HOCKEY!—HE BOUGHT HIS SKATES AND HIS HELMET YESTERDAY!

AND AS SOON AS HE GETS THE TIME—HE'S GOING TO TAKE HIM SKATING!

TED SAYS IT'S NO TROUBLE. HE SAYS HE'S ALWAYS WANTED A SON.

I WISH HE'D SAY A LITTLE MORE ABOUT WANTING A WIFE!

DO YOU WANT TO MARRY TED, CONNIE?

I WAS ALONE FOR SO LONG BEFORE HE CAME ALONG — I DON'T KNOW WHAT I WANT!

I GET FRUSTRATED WHEN HE'S AROUND TOO MUCH — BUT I GO CRAZY WHEN HE DOESN'T CALL.

I DON'T KNOW WHETHER I'M IN LOVE OR IN NEED.

Lynn

HEY, MA! GREG DAVIS GOT ROLLER SKATES! YEAH! ME AN' LAWRENCE WANT ROLLER SKATES

BUT, YOU WANTED TO PLAY HOCKEY! WE'VE ORDERED UNIFORMS AND BOUGHT ICE SKATES!!

WE CHANGED OUR MINDS!

I DON'T KNOW WHAT THEY'RE SO UPSET ABOUT. IT'S ONLY MONEY.

Lynn

MOM?

I THOUGHT YOU SAID WE'D BE ABLE TO WALK FASTER IF LIZZIE BROUGHT HER BIKE.

Lynn

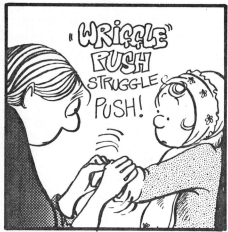

I WANT THAT, MOM! I WANT **THAT!** WANT DAT! WANT DAT! NO- I WANT-

MOM?-I WANT THAT. NIZZIE WANTS DAT! I WANT DAT! PLEASE? I WANT THAT! OK? I WANT THAT

I WANT THAT.

GRAMMA AN' GRAMPA PATTERSON ARE COMING FOR CHRISTMAS, LIZZIE! WANNA SEE THEM NOW!

THEY HAVE TO FLY ON A BIG PLANE ALL THE WAY FROM WINNIPEG, SO.... WANNA GO NOW! GO BIG PLANE!

LOOK, THEY'RE NOT COMING FOR A LONG TIME YET- WANNA SEE GAMMA **NOW!**

KIDS!

JOHN'S MOM AND DAD ARE COMING IN A COUPLE OF WEEKS AND I'VE HARDLY DONE A THING!

I HAVEN'T FINISHED MY SHOPPING, I HAVEN'T DONE MY CARDS OR MY PARCELS. I'M GOING NUTS!

ANNE- HOW DO YOU ALWAYS MANAGE TO STAY SO COOL AND COLLECTED IN THE MIDST OF CHAOS?

I EAT.

ALL RIGHT, ELVES! — I WANT ALL THE ELVES ON THIS SIDE, PLEASE.

CLAP CLAP

REINDEER? DO WE HAVE ALL 8 REINDEER? AND SANTA! — WHERE'S MICHAEL?

BOYS

NO, NO, ELVES! — YOU COME IN AFTER MRS. SANTA SAYS "MERCY ME, THE SLEIGH IS GONE!"

OK! — SINGING SNOW-FLAKES — WOULD YOU STAY IN LINE, PLEASE!

ANY MORE REINDEER CAUGHT FIGHTING WILL BE OUT OF THE SHOW!

MRS. HARDACRE? DO YOU THINK WE'LL EVER GET THIS TURKEY OFF THE GROUND?

WHY ARE YOU SO LATE, MICHAEL?

I HAD ANOTHER DETENTION.

WE WERE HAVING A DRESS REHEARSAL, AN' I SAID — HOW CAN THIS BE A DRESS REHEARSAL? — NOBODY'S WEARING A DRESS!

SO MRS. HARDACRE MADE ME STAY BEHIND AND PUT AWAY ALL THE COSTUMES.

SHE'S JUST GOT NO SENSE OF HUMAN!

HELLO, MRS. HARDACRE? THIS IS MICHAEL PATTERSON'S MOTHER. I WAS WONDERING IF WE COULD MEET AND HAVE A TALK ABOUT MICHAEL.

TOMORROW EVENING? YES, THAT'S FINE. I'LL BE THERE.

COME WITH ME?!!

YOU SEE, MICHAEL WOULD RATHER ENTERTAIN THE CLASS THAN GET HIS WORK DONE!

I UNDERSTAND. IT'S JUST THAT HE FEELS YOU'RE PICKING ON HIM.

OF COURSE I'M PICKING ON HIM!

I WOULDN'T BOTHER IF I DIDN'T THINK HE HAD POTENTIAL.

OH, NO! YOU TALKED TO MY TEACHER ABOUT ME?!

MICHAEL, SHE SAYS SHE'S STRICT WITH YOU BECAUSE YOU'RE BRIGHT AND SHE THINKS YOU COULD DO VERY WELL IF...

SHE PICKS ON ME 'CAUSE SHE THINKS I'M SMART?

BOY. AND THEY SAY THAT KIDS ARE HARD TO UNDERSTAND!

ISN'T DADDY COMING TO THE AIRPORT TO MEET GRAMMA, MOM?

NO, BUT HE'LL BE HOME WHEN WE GET BACK.

HOW COME WE'RE LEAVING SO EARLY? THE PLANE DOESN'T COME IN 'TILL 6!

I LIKE TO GIVE MYSELF TIME TO GET LOST ON THE FREEWAY.

AIR CANADA FLIGHT 81 FROM WINNIPEG IS NOW ARRIVING. PASSENGERS MAY BE MET AT THE M

STORIES

YAAY-GRAMMA AN' GRAMPA'S HERE! GAMMA! GAMPA!

HELLO THERE!

SHRIEK

AN' I GOT SKATES, AN' I'M IN GRADE 2 AN' I'M IN THE CHRISTMAS PLAY AN' GAMMA, LOOK!

I SINGING, MICHAEL! - SING LATER! - GRAMPA, I GOT THIS NEAT ROBOT, SEE - AN' ME AN' LAWRENCE - NIZZIE WANTS TO - LOOK! THERE'S OUR HOUSE!

DADDY! THEY'RE HERE!

SO...HOW ARE YOU?

".. AND HOPPITY HAMSTER HAD CHRISTMAS AFTER ALL.."

CLAP CLAP

DIDJA LIKE IT, GRAMPA? DIDJA SEE ME IN THERE?

WASN'T I A GOOD SANTA? DIDJA HEAR MY PART?

AREN'T GRANDPARENTS A WONDERFUL INVENTION!

UM... MRS HARDACRE?

UH.. I WANTED TO GIVE YOU THIS.

FOR ME, MICHAEL? OH, HOW VERY SWEET, DEAR!

GRAMMA SAID SHE'D BE HAPPY - BUT SHE NEVER TOLD ME I'D GET KISSED!

GRAMPA, WAS THERE A SANTA WHEN YOU WERE LITTLE?

OF COURSE! AND I SAT ON HIS KNEE - JUST LIKE YOU!

WAS HE EXACTLY THE SAME?

NOT EXACTLY.

HE WASN'T AS GENEROUS.

BLAMMO 49.95

BLAMMO 49.95

Cutesy Poo 27.50

10.95

AWW, GRANDMA— HOWCOME I GOTTA WEAR **THESE** BOOTS?

BECAUSE I FOUND TWO OF THEM.

MY GRANDMA AND GRAMPA ARE STAYING 'CAUSE MOM AN' DAD ARE GOING ON A HOLIDAY.

THEY'RE GOING AWAY FOR TWO WHOLE WEEKS!

BOY! TWO WHOLE WEEKS WITH YOUR GRAND-PARENTS, MIKE!

WHAT'S SO GOOD ABOUT THAT?

YOU'LL GET AWAY WITH MURDER!

SO—ANOTHER YEAR HAS ALMOST GONE BY!

YOU GOING TO MAKE ANY RASH NEW-YEARS' RESOLUTIONS?

NOPE, TED—DON'T HAVE TO.

MY WIFE MAKES THEM FOR ME.